Trade Binary Options Successfully :
A Complete Guide to Binary Options Trading

by A.J. Hakimi

For more free Binary Options guides see:
Binary Options Auto Trading Blog

Published by :
Hakimi bin Abdul Jabar (Binary Options Auto Trading Website & Blog)

Copyright © 2016 Hakimi bin Abdul Jabar. All Rights Reserved.

Table of Contents

1. The Single Most Critical Factor to Binary Options Trading Success (**page 2**)
2. What are Binary Options (**page 5**)
3. The Flow of Decisions in a Binary Options Trade (**page 7**)
4. Advantages and Disadvantages of Binary Options Trading (**page 12**)
5. Binary Trading Risk Management (**page 14**)
6. What You Need to Succeed in Binary Options (**page 17**)
7. How Much Money You Need to Start Trading (**page 20**)
8. Technical Analysis As a Tool for Binary Trading Success (**page 23**)
9. Developing a Binary Options Strategy and Entry Signals (**page 30**)
10. Trading Tips for Dessert (**page 35**)
11. Author's Biography (**page 36**)

1. The Single Most Critical Factor to Binary Options Trading Success

May I suggest that prior to reading this book you make yourself familiar with the look and feel of a real life Binary Options trading platform, this will help you to better understand the guidelines and concepts described here. You can simply register to an online broker, it is free and without any obligation on your part. Which broker? How about **this one** (**https://iqoption.com/promo/binary-options_en/?aff=38249**). This is the broker that we trade at, we chose it based on an extensive research and find it to be one of the best out there. I suggest you first tour its features and flip through the training resources in its extensive education center and just then commence with reading this book.

Now, there is one critical issue regarding Binary Options that I want to address right at the beginning of this guide and that is broker scam. In my opinion, the single most critical factor to your Binary Options trading success is that you trade with a honest and reliable broker. Why? because once you fall into the hands of a scamming broker, no matter how effective your strategies are, you are bound to lose all your money.

Now, the word must be said - Binary Options are a legitimate and a viable financial instrument and most binary options brokers are honest and reliable - however, there are a few bad apples out there that give others a bad name.

So how can you avoid falling prey to a scammer? Here are some ideas to help you with this.

For starter you can choose a broker from a list of regulated safe brokers. Such a list can be found at the **Binary Options Auto Trading Website & Blog** (https://binaryoptionsautotradingblog.wordpress.com/). The broker on this list has been checked and confirmed to be honest and trusted.

What if you want to trade with a broker that is not on the safe list? Here is a simple strategy that will help you choose a good broker. Once you decided to trade with a new broker, start small and watch for any irregularities in the behavior of his trading platform (see below). Trade with small amounts of money, test the waters first, once everything feels

OK and you are more confident with the broker, proceed with your planed amounts and strategy.

Now, How can you spot a scamming broker? I'm going to reveal to you now how a binary options scam works - once you know how it works it will be easy for you to identify it when it is being tried on you.

In a typical scam the broker manipulate the movements of the underlying asset, usually upon the expiry time, in a way that the outcome will be in favor of the broker. For example, If the binary option is supposed to expire at, say, 11h30 and at that time it is "in the money" (ITM), the option is manipulated to remain open until, say, 11h31, and that last minute may be just enough for your option to expire 'out of the money' (OTM).

According to one of the traders that was a victim to a scam, the broker has a system where you place a trade and a clock begins to count down to the expiration, when the clock ticks to zero you should be awarded a win or suffer a loss - until here this is a standard binary options trade, but listen what happens next. After the clock ticks to zero, you see this, "Expiring...." for at least another 30 to 60 seconds. During that time, if your trade was close, the stock move just enough for you to lose your money.

The scammer uses a trading platform where the trader has no way of having an exact time for the trade to expire because the clock goes to zero, but the broker keeps it open until it moves to where they get the investor's money.

Since this particular broker features the Reuters logo on its site, one of the complaining investors has been spoken with Reuters who has informed him that they are looking at opening a case against the scamming broker as he is a risk of being fraudulent and is using the Reuters name to big himself up.

Another complaining investor stated regarding this system of scam: "... I noticed that the web site used to track my trades was having issues with the trades actually expiring 30 to 60 seconds after the time had run out to zero. During this extra expiry time is when the strike amounts would move and I would not be awarded my winnings if they moved just enough for me

Copyright © 2016 Hakimi bin Abdul Jabar. All Rights Reserved.

to lose. Then the site started slowing and freezing so that I could not see my trades, track anything, or see information regarding possible trades."

In addition to observing the expiry time behavior of the brokers' trading platform you should also examine the behavior of the broker's asset's price movements during the contracts' time frame. You want to make sure the broker's chart follows the market accurately. You do this by comparing the broker's chart movements to a real-time chart of the same asset.

Now you know what to look for and how to identify a broker that uses scam techniques.

On a final note - there is one misconception about how binary options brokers make money that needs to be cleared. Some traders voiced concerns that they are trading "against the house" thus the brokers have an incentive to alter the data towards favorable outcomes for the broker. Well, this is not the case, a honest broker will derive his income from the difference between the total sum he pays to winning trades and the total sum that he gets from the losing trades.

Let's look at an example - this is simplified to make the point. Say there are only 2 trades, same asset, same time, same expiry time. One trader chooses 'Put' the other chooses 'Call'. Now the broker is indifferent as to what will be the outcome of the trade and which of the two traders win the trade, the broker's profit will come from the difference between what he gets from the loser and what he pays the winner.

You see, binary options brokers have a viable business model that is not dependant on the outcome of the trades. That's not to say that there are not a few dishonest brokers that are willing to defraud their customers for a dubious short term gain that will eventually cost them their business.

Copyright © 2016 Hakimi bin Abdul Jabar. All Rights Reserved.

2. What are Binary Options

The purpose of this guide is to show you how to make money trading Binary Options. In the first several chapters we will deal with the in and outs of binary options while later on we will go into the strategies needed to achieve success in trading binaries.

So what are Binary Options (also referred to as 'digital options', 'fixed return options' and 'all-or-nothing options')?

A binary option is In fact a prediction of which direction the price of the underlying asset
(a stock, commodity, index or currency) will move by a specified expiration time. With
Binary Options, an investor doesn't purchase the asset - he is merely predicting the direction that the underlying asset moves. There are actually just two possible outcomes. A fixed gain if the option expires "in the money", or a fixed loss if the option expires "out of the money." The price of the asset is not important. The only thing that is matter is whether the prediction is correct or incorrect.

A binary options trade usably involved three steps:

First, you choose a trade expiration time, this is the time you want the trade to end. It could be any time period between a minute and a week - usably it is within the day.

Second, you choose Call or Put. If you think the price will end up above the current price: you click the buy/call button. If you think the price will end up below the current price: click the sell/put button.

Now that the trade is placed, you simply wait for the outcome. If the trade expires 'in the money', you make a profit. If it expires 'out of the money', you'll lose.

Now you can see where the "binary" comes from, it stresses the fact that there are two possible outcomes to a binary option, both of which are set and understood by the investor prior to placing a trade.

Copyright © 2016 Hakimi bin Abdul Jabar. All Rights Reserved.

Now here is an example:

You purchase a Google binary option for $25, with the opinion that within 2 hours Google's shares will be higher than they currently stand. If you are correct you get a previously set percentage return on your investment (e.g. 82%), should the shares go lower you lose your investment (some brokers will give you back a small amount as a "refund").

A number of factors distinguish binary options from regular stock options.

Typically the short-run expiration time suggests traders could make an immediate profit on the binary options and therefore are way more versatile in their option investments.

In regular stock options, a trader will pay per contract. Therefore the investor may profit or lose a sum based on the quantity of points difference between the expiration level and the strike price. In contrast to binary options in which the two outcomes are actually set from the beginning.

An investor in a binary option needs to hold onto his option until the expiry date. He must consequently take more care when ever buying his options as he is unable to sell them after they are purchased.

Binary options are categorized as exotic options, however, inside financial markets they sometimes are termed as digital options. While digital options are quite simple to understand and easily traded, the mathematics behind the pricing is complex. It is because of this that digital options are referred to as exotic options.

For years Binary Options were traded by large institutions and their clients in the over the counter market (OTC). In 2008, the Securities and Exchange Commission in the US approved the listing of binary options with continuous quotations and now binary options are also available to individual investors.

Most binary options tracings nowadays are performed online thru private brokers that use sophisticated trading platforms.

3. The Flow of Decisions in a Binary Options Trade

A Binary Options trade calls for several decisions to be taken by the investor.

Deciding on the Underlying Asset

The first decision is choosing an asset. Based on which broker you decide on, you will have a selection of assets from different financial markets. Some traders elect to focus on one particular asset, or one market, while others trade several options simultaneously. One consideration as to what asset to trade has to do with the opening hours of the various world stock exchanges. Currencies are usably available for trade 24 hours a day.

Most brokers offers four classes of assets:

Commodities - e.g.: Gold, Silver, Wheat, Coffee, Oil, Sugar, Platinum.

Stocks - e.g.: City (US), Apple (US), Gazprom (Russia), BP (British Petroleum), Google (US), SberBank (Russia), Coca Cola(US).

Forex (Currencies) - e.g.: GBP/USD, USD/JPY, USD/CAD, EUR/JPY, EUR/GBP, USD/TRY, USD/CHF.

Indices (Indexes): - e.g.: DOW (US), S&P 500 (US), NASDAQ (US), DAX (Germany), CAC (France), FTSE 100 (U.K).

Deciding On an Amount to Invest

Binary options brokers allow for a low minimum so you can be flexible as to the amounts you can invest. The amounts you devote to trade should be dictated by your risk management plan (more on this when we talk about risk management later on).

Deciding On the Desired Time Frame

Binary options are short term investment instruments by definition. the time frame available can run from one minute to a week, depending on the trading platform.

So what time frame should you choose? The problem with selecting very small timeframes like one minute, or 5 minutes is that you could possibly experience a lot of "noise" which is a result of hedge funds activity, scalpers and automated trading. You could think that you observe an emerging trend only to realize that it was only a brief manipulated move and that the trend is over once you enter the market. Therefore I suggest you use at list a 15 minute time frame. This is small enough for you to capture the nice moves, but it's big enough to eliminate the noise in the market and correctly displays the "true trends."

While preparing a trading strategy (we will cover this in a later chapter), it is best to experiment with various timeframes. A trading strategy that doesn't work on a small timeframe might work on a larger timeframe and vice versa. Start developing your trading strategy using 15 minute timeframes, and if you're unhappy with the results simply experiment with other timeframes.

Deciding on the Type of Trade

Binary Options Trading Platforms allow for several trading types:

Above / Below

Above / Below is the most popular type of binary options trade, most traders will use this type the majority of the time. Above/Below options expire in-the-money when the trader correctly predicts that the price of the underlying asset will move above or below the predetermined strike price by the time of expiration.

Let's look at a trading example: while looking at the assets available for trading you choose Gold as the asset you would like to trade. Following an analysis (that we will discuss later on) you come to the conclusion that Gold is currently trending up.

Since you believe that the price of Gold will increase, you choose Call/up with an expiration time of 15 minutes and an amount of $100. You observe that the payout for this trade is 81%. If when the contract expires the price of Gold has risen, you'll finish in-the-money and take home the amount of $181.

Here's an example of an Above/Below trade:

Touch

With the Touch type options expire in-the-money if the price of the underlying asset touches a predetermined barrier by the time of expiration. Price barriers can be higher or lower than the current price of the underlying asset when the option is purchased.

Binary brokers also offer variations on Touch, including "Touch Up" and "Touch Down".

Let's look at a trading example: suppose you decide to trade a touch option on Google's stock. You select Google as the asset you would like to trade and see that the option is expiring in 15 minutes with a return of 71%. Depending on the current price of the asset, two options are available with predetermined strike prices, "Touch Up" and "Touch Down". You believe that the price of the underlying asset will touch the high strike price until the expiry date, so you select "Touch Up" and a trade amount of $100. On the other hand, if you believed that the price of Google would touch the low strike price, you would select "Touch Down".

If when the contract expires the price of Google has touched the option you selected, you'll finish in-the-money and take home a payout of $171.

Here's an example of a touch trade:

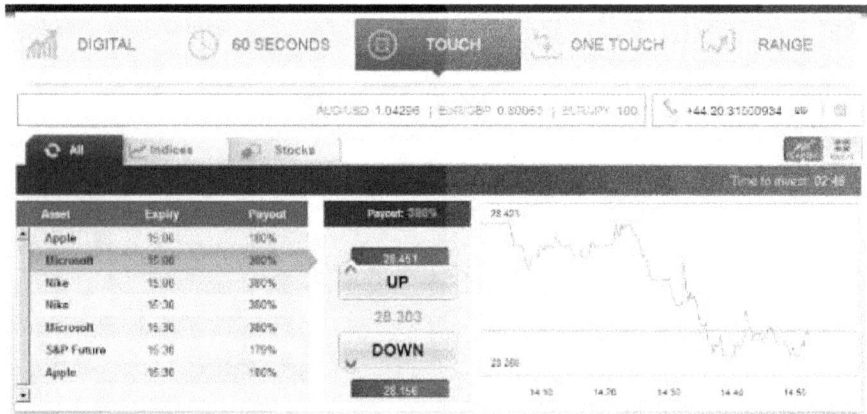

Range

Range options have a predetermined upper and lower boundary. When buying a range option, the trader have to predict whether the price of the underlying asset will stay "In" or go "Out" of a predetermined range at the time of expiration. in a range option you can trade on the volatility of the asset. If you think that the asset volatility is high, you will choose an "Out" of the range option. On the other hand, if you think that the option is not volatile, you will buy an "In" range option.

Let's look at a trading example: You decide to trade a Forex option, USD/EUR. You see that there are two options available, "In" and "Out". Each option has a predetermined range and you must determine if the asset will be in the upper or lower range at the time of expiration.

Based on your analysis you think that the price of the USD / EUR will be in the range at the time of expiration so you select the "In" option. If you thought that the price would be out of the range at the time of expiration, you should have bought an "Out" option.

If when the contract expires the price of USD / EUR stayed in the predetermined range that you selected, you'll get the predetermined payout amount

Additional Features

Some brokers will allow for some variations on the trading types. This may include: 'Close Now' and 'Extend'. Note that both features require that you pay a flat fee upon implementing.

Close Now - this feature allows you to sell your option before the time of expiration. This enables you to close an option before the time of expiration if it isn't performing as planned.

Extend (Roll Over) - allows you to extend the time of expiration in order to increase the odds of being in-the-money.

4. Advantages and Disadvantages of Binary Options Trading

Consider the following advantages and disadvantages when trading Binary Options:

Advantages

Risk control - With binary options the return on initial investment is fixed From the beginning, thus the amount of possible profit or loss is well known. Which means that you'll never lose more than what you expected and can determine your risk as completely as is possible. There's a limit on how much could be earned or lost in one trade. Because the rate of return is relatively high, and trade times are short, in the long run the fixed rate of a binary option can be a big advantage.

Short-time trading (daily, hourly) – with binary options you decide what the expiry time of the option will be. If you are a fan of long-time investments, you can choose "end of the week" and "end of the month" expiry times. However, most traders would prefer shorter time frames.

Low minimum amounts – Binary brokers have low investment minimums, thus allowing you to start with small amounts. With IQ OPTION you can start trading with as low as USD$1 with a minimum trading deposit of USD$10. If you are familiar with stock market trading, you probably know that you need a decent amount of preliminary investment capital, brokers, commissions, etc. Thus the possibility to begin trading with just $10 as well as the flexibility to pick your investment amount is certainly an advantage.

Online trading – binary options are traded on online platforms and therefore you don't need any software downloads. Trading is available from anywhere, all you need is a computer and internet access. You simply enter your login and password and get straight to your personal profile page and start trading.

Simplicity - Trading Binary Options is very simple and straightforward, all you need to do is decide which of the two directions the asset will move, up or down.

Disadvantages

The main disadvantage of trading binary options is the level of "fee" that is paid to the broker, it is relatively higher than in other investment areas. Fee? What fee? Well, it's not exactly a fee, it's more of a 'spread'. The brokers' "fee" is embedded in the business model of a binary options brokerage. You buy the options contracts from the broker, if you win, the broker will pay you out about 71% to 85%. If the contract expires "out of the money", some brokers will refund a small percentage of the principal. The broker gets the difference between the sum that they keep on a losing trade and the amount they pay out on a winning trade.

5. Binary Trading Risk Management

Your first concern when trading binary options should be not to risk too much money on any given trade. Unfortunately, many traders start trading binaries without thinking about the risk that they are taking - only about the potential rewards.

If you want to succeed in binary trading you must take into consideration the maximum percentage of the total trading money that you should risk in any one trade. Actually, your ability to limit your losses is equally as critical (or even more critical) as your success in managing winning trades.

The goal of practicing a good binary options money management is to minimize risk and increase payouts. For starters here are 3 quick tips:

First, Trading binary options is fun and exciting and money can be made; but you must also keep in mind that like with any other options trading there is the risk of losing.
Hence, binary options trading rule number one: do not trade with money you can't afford to lose.

Second, never borrow money while trading, trade only with your own money.

And third, set and stick to a budget. Write it on your forehead if you have to, but no matter what, when you hit that number, quit trading for the day.

Good money management calls for adopting a conservative investment strategy that means that you should never risk your entire capital.

When you enter a trade (no matter how great it may be), always ensure to only invest conservatively. By conservative I mean that you should not use more than 5% of your capital on any single trade. Binary options trading like any other stock investing is not a sure thing, there is always a risk factor involved. A conservative investment strategy helps you to conserve your money when things go wrong.

Binary options trading offers a lot of choices to the trader. A good money management strategy requires diversification. The volatility that accompanies trading currency pairs is much distinct from say trading commodities as well as stocks. Obviously, the payouts may vary depending on the asset which is selected. As the saying goes, never put all your eggs in the same basket.

Losses in a trade should be accepted on a positive note. The effects of a trade that goes against you are able to impact the future or successive trade decisions. Expecting losses whilst investing, whether it is Forex trading or binary options can assist traders in identifying the areas which may happen to be unnoticed. Losses needs to be seen as a stepping stone instead of having it affect you.

Start off slow and scale up - this has a significant role particularly for beginner traders.

Certainly do not fall for the emotions and commit your entire amounts right away on one trade. Investing in small amounts continually helps you to take a self-disciplined approach. The majority of binary options brokers allow for a minimum trade sum between $10 and $30. Use this advantage and be sure to trade with patience.

Do not expect to make gains with binary options trading as soon as you made your first deposit. No matter if you commit $100 or $3000 the exact same key facts apply. Trade in small amounts until you have the sense of the assets that you're trading. This can gradually build your self-confidence levels and helps to automatically be aware of the indicators and be able to prepare your investing strategy and ultimately help reduce the losses. One of the important things that specifies successful traders has to do with using a good money management strategy.

The above strategy has now became something of an accepted mainstream investment theory and is an ideal method on which to found your own binary options money management strategy.

As we mentioned before the money management strategy that we recommend is using no more than 5% of your entire budget in any one trade. The idea behind this approach is to achieve optimum growth while minimizing the risk. Simply put, the biggest downfall to producing good results in binary options derives from the risks involving losing.
Therefore if you are able to reduce these risks, you'll have a far better chance of making money with your account to come.

Now how would this work in the real world? Let us have a look at an example: Beginning capital $1000, Thus 5% will amount to $50 per binary contract placed in your account.

With a typical binary options broker this could equal 5% risked for a possible 3.5% return, supposing a 70% pay out. While this might appear low to some binary investors, keep in mind that this method concentrates on risk reduction and capital generation as a way to maximize long-term growth potential.

By adopting this approach you can take a 'hit' on your account and still endure a chain of losses. Actually you can tolerate a run of 20 losing trades prior to your balance hit zero.

There is a fine line between gambling and trading. To 'gamble' is to take a high risk with limited chance of achieving your expected pay out. To 'trade' is to take a calculated risk which will nevertheless provide you with a good return as well as keep you in the game for the long run.

Not only will pursuing this kind of strategy truly enable you to improve your outcomes, it will as well help your mental well being. When starting any type of trading you shouldn't be in a position in which you are sweating on a contract winning.

Aiming and sticking with a strategy which offers successful money management does not just make sure you are not kept up at nighttime; it will as well make sure that a loss will not signal the end of your investing career.

6. What You Need to Succeed in Binary Options

Binaries are simple to trade but don't make the mistake of thinking that they are easy to make money with. There are many websites that tell you differently. They make you think that you just have to sign up for an account, start trading and ...voila, become a successful trader. Well, life is not that easy.

Like in many other areas, you need a solid knowledge before you get started. Hopefully you'll get some of it here in this guide. Be aware, though, that just reading this guide will not automatically make you an instant millionaire. You'll learn a lot of facts and strategies about binary trading, but in order to make the most out of this guide and become the trader you want to be, you'll have to adapt the ideas that you're about to learn to what you already know.

For starters you need to learn how to read the charts. Charts are your main weapon in winning the Binary Options wars - ...well, maybe I'm a bit melodramatic here. But seriously, charts are a vital resource for a serious binary trader, actually any valid strategy involves reading and analyzing charts.

Basically, the charts allow you to predict the future course of an asset by finding patterns in its past price movements, and after all this what we need to win a binary trade.

Don't be intimidated by the charts, actually they are not that hard to read and understand. Strategies that are based on reading and analyzing charts are part of the technical analysis area.

Technical analysis follows a straightforward set of rules freely available on scores of websites. Happily, the simplest rules in charting tend to be the most reliable. In a later chapter we will go over several strategies that you can apply in your trades.

The most basic form of technical analysis would be to look for support and resistance levels that markets have struggled to break through in the past. Charts in this way works best in moderately volatile markets. Technical analysis is also useful in identifying trending assets.

Another simple way of using charts is to look at moving averages, such as the average price over 10 days. The idea is that this gives you a better representation of what the price is doing over a longer period of time.

Copyright © 2016 Hakimi bin Abdul Jabar. All Rights Reserved.

Another simple pattern is based on the so-called relative strength index (RSI). This highlights situations where a market is overbought or oversold and warns of a potential reversal in the trend. The RSI is the total points gained on up days, divided by the total points lost and gained, multiplied by 100.

Now that you are convicted in the necessity of charts the question is where can you get them. Well, there are a lot of online charts services and software, to find them simply run an online search for "real time charts" or "charts software".

Effective charting service packages help you access the market data in real-time; this information is shown in a number of ways, which will help you in performing your trades.

Finding the "right" charting service is definitely a personal choice - it could be compared to selecting the right car. What another trader prefers could be not the same as what you select, and the other way round. That is the reason why it may be necessary for you to properly examine a list of features - with both pros and cons - prior to making the decision on a charting service.

In essence you must have a list of criteria, and you have to compare the available charting services using that list. Make your selection based on the results. Listed below are requirements you should consider:

Real-Time Data - You want a reliable system that will provide real-time information immediately. This particular feature by itself will leave out many of the options available, because a lot of online packages will have some kind of delay. With regards to binary trading you obviously can't afford to face a delay.

Market Data Coverage - Look at markets which are included in the charting service. The majority of programs include the major U.S. markets, but if you have to have other global markets, like Asian or European markets, then you definitely have to make sure that data is available in real-time.

Variety of Indicators - Based on your own personal requirements, you may be interested in a diverse variety of indicators and charting methods, such as bar charts, point-and - figure charting, or Japanese candlesticks. Additionally, find out if the charting service can show basic indicators like MACD, RSI, and Moving Averages easily (I will explain all these later). If you're serious about technical analysis, ensure that you can easily program your own indicators or modify the existing ones to your desires without having too much trouble.

Reasonably competitive Rates - You will need a charting service that won't cost you all of your money before you even get into your first trade. It's necessary to shop around. Nonetheless, locating a competitive price is not to mean that the provider's service is the cheapest. You need to be cautious with this one - the old saying "you get what you pay for" certainly does apply with regards to trading. Consider your choices. You seldom want cheap trading service that gives you next to nothing, however, you probably don't need the most expensive service with options you won't make use of - either. And make sure that the company you choose will allow time to test out how the service really works. Should you be not comfortable with using it, you should be able to ask for a refund.

User Friendly Platform - You need to have a system that you can use easily, not one that needs a degree as a computer engineer. You'll need a system that lets you back-test strategies and program customized indicators and trading systems without a lot of difficulty.

Reputable Company - Pick a reputable provider which has a recognized reputation online for its platform and data feed. And obviously, select a provider which has superb customer service.

I hope at this point you have a much better notion of what sort of charting service can best meet your needs. Keep in mind, effective charting application is actually what will give you the velocity and ability to perform fast trades in response to breaking news.

Over time, you may want to move on to more sophisticated services as you become more skilled in the investing universe.

7. How Much Money You Need to Start Trading

Naturally, you will need capital to trade. Nevertheless you've likewise heard this warning more than once: "Don't trade with money that you can't afford to lose." You may think this is simply the conventional warning that each pro inside the investing field needs to use. But it is certainly not. It is a lot more.

There is more to trading than simply using a strategy. A trader's two major enemies are fear and greed. This is very often the case. That is why controlling your feelings is extremely important to your trading.

It is extremely important not to place excessive strain on yourself or your trading performance. And to maintain the stress down, you most likely should not quit your day job just yet. Prior to being a skilled binary trader, your trading should be consistent, and your gains ought to be nearly foreseeable. Provide yourself some time to prove that you have what it takes to trade for a living.

Regarding the sum of money you really need, that depends on you. Possessing too much money in your trading account could be equally as harmful as having too little. If you have $100,000 in your trading account and only risk $ 100 per trade, you may think of your losses as 'peanuts.' Even though we have to learn to accept losses as part of the business, we have to still by no means consider them as 'peanuts!' There is a balance. You need to find it.

You must fund your account properly - not too much and not too little. And be ready for a period of time where you might not generate a lot of money with it. As with everything, there exists a learning process when it comes to trading.

Numerous newbie traders believe they ought to trade all of their savings. This is obviously a dangerous belief. In order to find out the amount of money you should trade with, you must first identify just how much you can actually afford to lose, and what your financial goals are.

We need to start by identifying just how much of your savings need to stay in your savings account. It is very important to always keep three to six months of living expenses in an easily accessible savings account, therefore set that money apart, and don't trade it! You must never trade money that you could need immediately. The rest of the sum of money will probably be what you currently have to trade with.

Have a look at the amount of money you can presently afford to trade. You rarely want other parts of your life to suffer when you tie your money up in a trade, so ensure that you consider what these savings were originally for.

Next, figure out how much you can contribute to your trading activities in the future. In case you are presently employed, you will continue to receive an income, and you can plan to make use of a part of that income to build your investment portfolio over time.

Two more important things to keep in mind: most brokers require a minimum deposit of $100 to $200, so this sets a minimum initial amount that you need to start trading with. This does not mean that you will be risking the whole amount in one trade, as discussed previously try to restrict each trade to no more than 5% of your account size.

Another subject that needs to be considered is your risk tolerance. Everyone has a risk tolerance which should not be overlooked.

Identifying one's risk tolerance requires a number of different factors. To begin with, you should know what amount of cash you have to invest, and what your investment and financial goals are.

As an illustration, if you plan on retiring in ten years, and you haven't saved a single penny yet, you are getting to have to have a higher risk tolerance, simply because you'll have to do some aggressive trading to be able to achieve your financial target. On the other side of the coin, if you're in your early twenties and you wish to begin investing for your retirement, your risk tolerance could be lower. You are able to afford to observe your money grow gradually with time.

Understand, naturally, that your need for a higher risk tolerance or your need for a low risk tolerance have no bearing on how you feel about risk. Once again, there exists a lot in identifying your tolerance. For example, if you entered a trade, and you see that trade go against you, what would you do? Let's say you are hit with a $ 1000 loss. Would you keep on trading, or would you call it off for the day? If you have a low tolerance for risk, you would want to stop trading for the day. If you have a high tolerance, you would keep on trading.

This kind of decision is not depending on what your financial goals are. This tolerance is based on how you feel about your money. And, naturally, your account size plays a vital role in determining your risk tolerance. In case you have a $2,000 account, then a $1,000 loss will make you nervous, as you are shedding 50% of your investment capital.

But if your trading account size is $100,000, and you are faced with a $1,000 loss, then you might be more calm, as it is just 1% of your account.

Copyright © 2016 Hakimi bin Abdul Jabar. All Rights Reserved.

As you'll learn, emotions are a very important element in trading; for that reason, it's important to take the time to figure out your risk tolerance.

8. Technical Analysis As a Tool for Binary Trading Success

In order to be able to develop effective binary options strategies you need to understand technical analysis. This chapter is design to acquaint you with the basic terms and concepts of technical analysis.

So what is Technical Analysis?

Basically, technical analysis is the studying of investor behavior as well as its influence on the price action of financial instruments. The primary information which we have to carry out our studies would be the price histories of the instruments, along with time and volume data. All these allow us to make our predictions, depending on objective data.

Technical analysis keeps track of and analyzes the ways by which investors behave. This kind of behavior is collectively called sentiment. Technical analysts' viewpoint is that investor sentiment would be the single most important factor in identifying an instrument's price. Technical analysis practitioners believe that this analysis holds the real key to tracking investor sentiment.

In technical analysis we use charts to predict asset price movement and develop our strategies, this is why it is extremely important that you will be knowledgeable as to the various charts types that are being used in technical analysis.

Generally there are numerous ways to present price charts. Each has its unique advantages, however overall it is up to the person to determine which offers the best visual picture and is likely to be of most in discovering trends early on. We will look at the most widely used four types utilized by the pros:

Line Charts

This is actually the most basic chart format and is produced simply by using a line to join the data points.

The most typical use for line charts is for indicators that just have a single daily value (as opposed to high/low) for instance momentum or moving averages.

Here's a sample of a line chart:

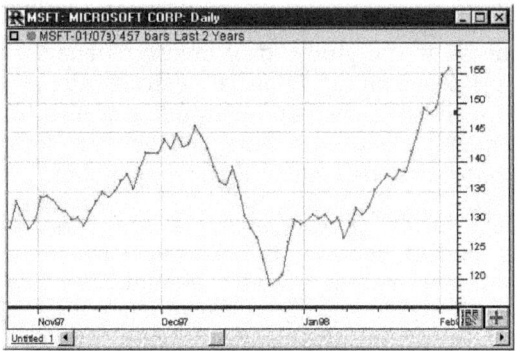

Bar Charts

Bar charts use vertical bars to show the price action of the underlying asset for a specific day, it indicates the lower and the higher price for the day.

As their name suggests, bar charts use vertical bars to represent price action for that day, drawn from the lowest price to the highest price.

Bar charts have indicators for the high and the low price of the asset. The left hand "notch" indicates the opening price of the asset and the right hand "notch" indicates the closing price.

Bar charts scales can be modified to show daily, weekly or monthly bars.

Here is a sample of a bar chart:

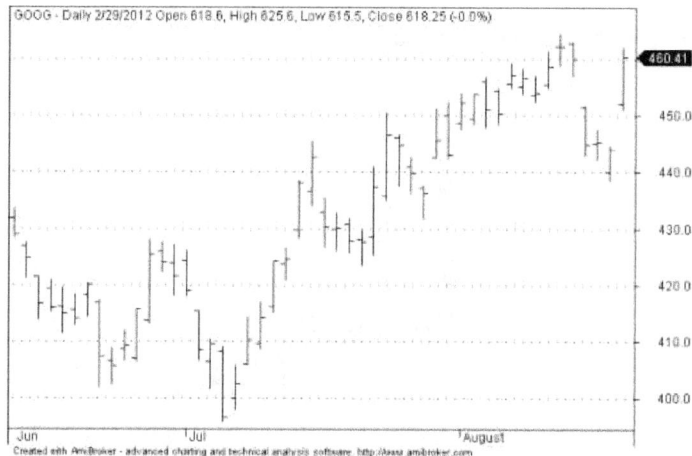

Candlestick Charts

Candlestick charts offer a more detailed visual representation of bar charts. The opening price is included in the chart and a day's activity would be represented as follows: an up day is indicated by a white (or empty) box. A down day is indicated by a black or shaded box. The "box" shows the open to close range. The "wick" displays the full day's range.

Candlestick charts are generally plotted over a one-day period but technical analysts also use weekly and monthly candlestick charts to provide a valuable picture of the longer-term price action.

Candlestick charting is one of the oldest methods of technical analysis, with Japanese and Chinese both claiming that rice traders were using candlestick charts over 4000 years ago. Candlestick appeal lies in its ability to give a clear visual representation of the price action during a period, leading to easy-to-recognize pattern recognition.

Here is a sample of a candlestick chart:

Support and Resistance

Being familiar with the models of support and resistance is essential in creating a disciplined binary trading strategy. Prices are dynamic, highlighting the ongoing change in the balance between supply and demand. By determining the price levels at which of these balances change we are able to plan the price level where to buy. Even though these levels could be created by the markets subconsciously they signify the collective views of the individuals in the markets.

Support represents the level where buying pressure is powerful enough to absorb and overcome the selling pressure. At price support levels buyers move into the market mopping up the imbalance between supply (sellers) and demand (buyers) so that when this happens the price will stop its fall and may probably rise.

Resistance is the opposite of support and is the level where the volume of selling (supply) exceeds the volume of buying (demand). These mini-levels may change frequently but over time a visible pattern comes out and firm levels come to be set up.

Here is a sample of support and resistant levels:

Copyright © 2016 Hakimi bin Abdul Jabar. All Rights Reserved.

The Concept of Trend

We all know that prices do not rise or fall in a straight line but rather move in a series of zigzags which resembled waves. Now, the relative positioning of the peaks and troughs in these waves define the trend.

For a stock to be in an uptrend, it must make successive higher peaks (highs) and higher troughs (lows). For a stock to be in a downtrend, it must make lower peaks
(highs) and lower troughs (lows).

Simply by figuring out these types of peaks and troughs, we are able not just to explain the present trend and set it in its historic framework but, equally as important, figure out when it is changing. We do this by looking at the patterns created by the peaks and troughs.

Here's an example of a trend:

Copyright © 2016 Hakimi bin Abdul Jabar. All Rights Reserved.

Moving Averages

The moving average is probably the most widely used indicator and is used by technical analysts for numerous sorts of tasks. Moving averages can be used to discover regions of short term support/resistance, to look for the current trend and as a component in numerous other indicators like the MACD, or Bollinger bands.

The primary benefits of moving averages is first of all that they smooth the data and therefore offer a sharper visible picture of the present trend and subsequently, that moving average signals can provide an accurate answer as to what the trend is. The primary downside is that they are lagging rather than leading indicators.

There are actually two major types of moving average:

The simple moving average calculates the average price over a specific moving time period. For example, a 50 day simple moving average will calculate the average mean price from the last 50 days closing prices..

The exponential moving average also averages the last x days closes but designates a greater weight to the more recent prices which makes it more sensitive to present price action thereby decreasing the lag impact.

Here's an example of moving averages:

Copyright © 2016 Hakimi bin Abdul Jabar. All Rights Reserved.

9. Developing a Binary Options Strategy and Entry Signals

The Binary Options strategies featured here are based on technical analyses. This guide is intended to serve as a primer and a starting point. To take full advantage of these strategies you need a level of technical analysis knowledge that is beyond the scope of this guide. However, you can easily find information online to complement your knowledge. Once you want to apply any of the strategies listed here simply run a Google search using the title of the strategy as the search term and you'll find plenty of information that will allow you to obtain the knowledge you need to put that strategy into effect.

The Moving Averages Strategy

Moving averages gives you a hint as to the direction of the market, this is useful in identifying a trend. A trend is a good entry signal. A disadvantage of moving averages is that they tend to leg the market thus you need to use short period moving averages, such as a 5- or 6-day moving average, to reflect the current price action.

Moving averages are the most basic and most utilized technical indicator. They are used for smoothing the price movement. Moving averages are used as a trend line which adapts to price changes, not just as a regular trend line.

The Moving Averages strategy gives you the following signals:

If the closing price moves above the moving average - this is a buy signal.

If the closing price dips below the moving average - this a sell signal.

The Crossover of Moving Averages Strategy

Crossover of Moving Averages is another strategy that can help you identify a trend. This comprises of two moving averages: a "fast" moving average (e.g. 10 bars) and a "slow" moving average (e.g. 15 bars). The slow-moving average needs to use a larger amount of days than the fast one.

A crossover is regarded as a basic form of signal and is preferred amongst numerous investors since it eliminates all emotion. The standard kind of crossover is when the price of an asset moves from one side of a moving average and closes on the other.

Price crossovers are employed by investors to spot changes in momentum and can be used as a simple entry strategy. A close above a moving average from below may suggest the beginning of a new uptrend.

The Crossover of Moving Averages Strategy gives you the following signals:

When the fast-moving average crosses the slow moving average from below - that's a buy signal.

When the fast moving average crosses the slow moving average from above - that's a sell signal.

Here's a sample of moving averages crossover

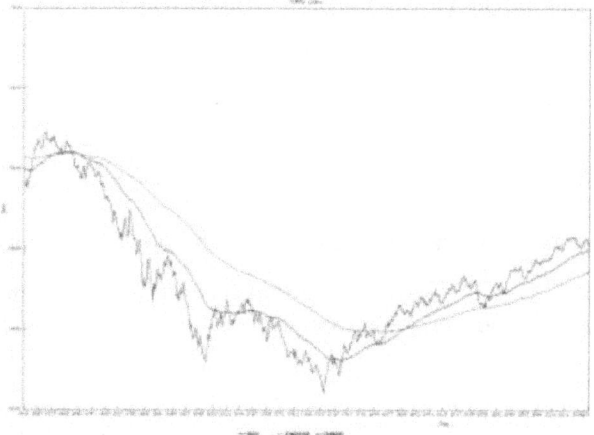

The Turtle Trading Strategy

The Turtle Trading strategy is quite popular among many traders, search the internet for explanations as to how to make full use of it. In essence, the turtles evaluate the high and the low over the past 20 days.

The Turtle Trading Strategy gives you the following signals:

When the current prices move higher than the high of the previous 20 bars - that's a buy signal.

When the current prices move lower than the low of the previous 20 bars - that's a sell signal.

The Moving Average Convergence Divergence Strategy (MACD)

The MACD strategy is another indicator that is useful in identifying trends. This indicator take advantage of the relationship between two moving averages of prices.

Most traders use the difference between a 26-bar exponential moving average (EMA) and the 12-bar. This difference is then plotted on the chart and oscillates above and below zero. A 9-bar EMA of the MACD, called the "signal line," is then plotted on top of the MACD, functioning as a trigger for buy and sell signals.

The MACD strategy can be used in various ways, however the most popular is to use the signal line for entry signals as follows:

When the signal line crosses the MACD from below - that's a buy signal.

When the signal line crosses the MACD from above - That's a sell signal.

The Williams Percent Range Indicator Strategy (Williams %R)

The Williams %R strategy developed in 1966 by Larry Williams. Its purpose is to help identify overbought and oversold positions in the market.

This indicator is categorized as an "oscillator" because the values vary between zero and "-100". The indicator chart usually has lines drawn at both the "-20" and "-80" values as alert signals. Values between "-80" and "-100" are interpreted as a strong oversold condition, or "selling" signal, and between "-20" and "0.0", as a strong overbought condition, or "buying" signal.

The Williams %R strategy gives you the following signals:

When the indicator has a value above 80 - that's a sell signal.

When the indicator has a value below 20 - that's a sell signal.

Relative Strength Index Strategy (RSI)

The Relative Strength Index strategy is yet another overbought/oversold signal. it was created by Welles Wilder.

The goal of the Relative Strength Index (RSI) is to determine the comparative changes that occur between the higher and the lower closing prices. The index is used by traders to determine overbought conditions and oversold conditions which then provides them with highly useful info to help establish entry points and exit points of the underlying asset. The RSI is an oscillator and its line 'oscillates' between the values of zero and one hundred. The values of 70 and 30 are viewed as significant values since above and below them are the overbought and oversold areas respectively. Just about any value above 84 is regarded as a very strong overbought situation and produces a 'sell' signal, while every value below 15 is regarded as quite a solid oversold situation and produces a 'buy' signal.

The Relative Strength Index Strategy gives you the following signals:

When the RSI crosses the 70-line, overbought-zone, from above - that's a sell signal.

When the RSI crosses the 30-line, oversold zone, from below- that's a buy signal.

The Bollinger Bands and Channels Strategy

"Bollinger Bands" incorporate a moving average and two standard deviations, one above the moving average and one below. The main thing to understand about Bollinger Bands is that they consist of up to 95% of the closing prices, according to the settings.

Trading Bollinger Bands can assist you to fully grasp a number of characteristics of an asset such as the high or low of the day, whether a stock is trending, as well as whether it is volatile or stable. Sometimes while trading Bollinger bands, you will notice the bands coiling really tightly which indicates the stock is trading in a narrow range. This is actually the trigger to look at for a price breakout or breakdown. Often large rallies start from low volatility ranges. When this occurs, it is termed as "building cause", this is actually the calm before the storm.

Copyright © 2016 Hakimi bin Abdul Jabar. All Rights Reserved.

The Bollinger Bands Strategy gives you the following signals:

When prices move above the upper Bollinger Band - that's a sell signal.

When prices move below the lower Bollinger Band from below - that's a buy signal.

Here's a sample of Bollinger bands

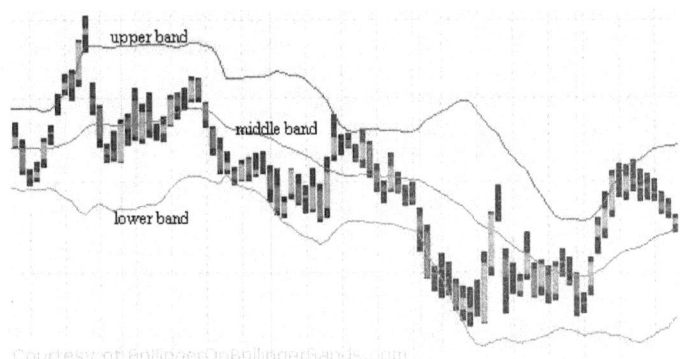

Trading the News Strategy

The market is influenced by news events and by learning how to take advantage of these events you can improve your profits and prevent expensive mistakes. Many beginner binary option traders come to recognize the significance of news events only after seeing a perfectly profitable trade becomes a loss in a few minutes, while skilled binary traders foresee the move and add to their daily gains in a regular manner.

Economic news reports usually initiate solid short-term moves in the assets markets which could create trading opportunities for traders. Announcements about corporate profits, a change in management, rumors of a merger, are all events which could result in a corporate entity's share price to move significantly up or down. Interest rates, unemployment and export rates, or the central bank's policy changes, can lead to a serious change of an exchange rate. So how can you trade this strategy? Simply follow the news closely and act fast. A good news event is a buy signal while a bad news event is a sell signal.

Copyright © 2016 Hakimi bin Abdul Jabar. All Rights Reserved.

10. Trading Tips for Dessert

1. Before implementing any strategy you must check for any related news events. Why? because news events may interfere with your strategy and distort the outcome that you are expecting. Bad news may cause an uptrend to swing down and good news may cause a downtrend to swing up. Before implementing any trade simply run an online search to make sure there are no adverse news events expected.
2. Different parts of the day coincide with different amounts of volatility in the market.
   For example, the afternoon, when no major announcements are expected, will be associated with less volatility than the morning hours. Thus, trade volatility (Range Out) before noon and stability (Range In) afternoon.
3. You can expect the market to get volatile and make large swings right after major market announcements such as interest rate announcements by the fed and job reports.
4. Trading stocks times is subject to the opening hours of the relevant stock exchanges. Obtain a table with the trading hours of the various world bourses.
5. Have a trading plan and a strategy and always stick to them.
6. Take time to improve your technical analysis knowledge, this will help you to sharpen your strategies.
7. Control your emotions and never trade when you are tired or drunk, this may lead to irrational behavior and losses. Always trade while you are relaxed and focused.
8. For trades with expiration times shorter than one day use 5 minute charts to establish your entry points.
9. While trading, your main concern should be limiting risk and protecting your capital. Develop a money management plan and stick to it, always!
10. Define your entry points. This is a part of developing and following your trading plan.
    Don't trade without having a trading plan.

*****

With this we conclude this guide. I hope you find it helpful and wish you success with your binary trading!

Copyright © 2016 Hakimi bin Abdul Jabar. All Rights Reserved.

Author's Biography

An alumnus of High School Batu Pahat/Hi-Skool. A graduate alumnus of the University of Wolverhampton, LLB (Hons) July 1998. Certificate in Legal Practice of Malaysia graduate, October 2000. Admitted and enrolled as an Advocate & Solicitor of the High Court of Malaya at Kuala Lumpur, Malaysia, on 24th. January 2002. A practising lawyer till December 31st. 2005 and former active member of the Malaysian Bar as a pro bono Legal Aid Programme volunteer lawyer at the Kuala Lumpur Legal Aid Centre at Wisma Kraftangan & MCA Public Services and Complaints Department volunteer legal advisor at Wisma MCA. A former legal officer in the Prosecution and Litigation Division of the Employees Provident Fund Board of Malaysia. A former manager at Citigroup Sales and Outsourcing Services Sdn. Bhd. A fulltime writer for years till present. A single childless bachelor. A singer, songwriter, composer, lyricist by the name of A.J. Hakimi, who has produced musical singles such as "Mama, Don't Cry!" and "The Joy of Peace". IQ OPTION Affiliate.

A Harvard University [HarvardX] certified Humanitarian Responder.

https://courses.edx.org/certificates/6b03e25779f24b18bbba917ee5f1acc1

https://www.amazon.com/Hakimi-Abdul-Jabar/e/B016X204PE

https://itunes.apple.com/us/artist/a.j.-hakimi/id1112480699

https://play.spotify.com/album/68OOWsn0x9VJaWCwByTtJp?play=true&utm_source=open.spotify.com&utm_medium=open

https://binaryoptionsautotradingblog.wordpress.com/

http://hakimibinabduljaba.wixsite.com/podcastmaestro

Copyright © 2016 Hakimi bin Abdul Jabar. All Rights Reserved.

www.ingramcontent.com/pod-product-compliance
Lightning Source LLC
Chambersburg PA
CBHW061235180526
45170CB00003B/1306